D1087883

# VOICES OF WAR

# The Civil War
## The War Between Brothers

**Enzo George**

Cavendish
Square
New York

Published in 2015 by Cavendish Square Publishing, LLC
243 5th Avenue, Suite 136, New York, NY 10016

First Edition

Website: cavendishsq.com

This publication represents the opinions and views of the author based on his or her personal experience, knowledge, and research. The information in this book serves as a general guide only. The author and publisher have used their best efforts in preparing this book and disclaim liability rising directly or indirectly from the use and application of this book.

CPSIA Compliance Information: Batch #WS14CSQ

All websites were available and accurate when this book was sent to press.

Library of Congress Cataloging-in-Publication Data
George, Enzo.
The Civil War: the war between brothers / by Enzo George.
p. cm. — (Voices of war)
Includes index.
ISBN 978-1-62712-858-2 (hardcover) ISBN 978-1-62712-860-5 (ebook)
1. United States — History — Civil War, 1861-1865 — Juvenile literature. 2. United States — History — Civil War, 1861-1865. I. Title.
E468.G46 2015
973.7—d23

For Brown Bear Books Ltd:
Editorial Director: Lindsey Lowe
Managing Editor: Tim Cooke
Children's Publisher: Anne O'Daly
Design Manager: Keith Davis
Designer: Lynne Lennon
Picture Manager: Sophie Mortimer
Production Director: Alastair Gourlay

Manufactured in the United States of America

# CONTENTS

Introduction ........................................4

Joining Up ........................................6

Training ........................................8

"Johnny Reb" ........................................10

"Billy Yank" ........................................12

The First Battle ........................................14

Battle of the Ironclads ........................................16

Life on Campaign ........................................18

Life in the Cavalry ........................................20

In a Firefight ........................................22

Under Siege ........................................24

The Union Home Front ........................................26

Home Front in the South ........................................28

The African-American Experience ........................................30

The Bloodiest Day ........................................32

The Battle of Gettysburg ........................................34

Medicine and Nursing ........................................36

Recreation and Entertainment ........................................38

Discipline and Punishment ........................................40

Lee's Surrender ........................................42

The Death of Lincoln ........................................44

Glossary ........................................46

Further Information ........................................47

Index ........................................48

# Introduction

When Abraham Lincoln was elected as president in 1860, the United States was split between North and South. Southerners were worried that he would outlaw slavery, which was illegal in the North. In December 1860, South Carolina seceded from, or quit, the Union. Ten more states followed, and together they set up the Confederate States of America.

Lincoln went to war to reunite the Union. At first, both sides thought the war would be short. But after Confederate troops defeated the Union at the First Battle of Bull Run (Manassas) in July 1861, it became clear that the war would be long and costly.

*Union drummer Gilbert A. Marbery of the 22nd New York Infantry poses next to a cannon.*

*Union troops (left) clash with Confederates in the Battle of Winchester in Virginia in May 1862.*

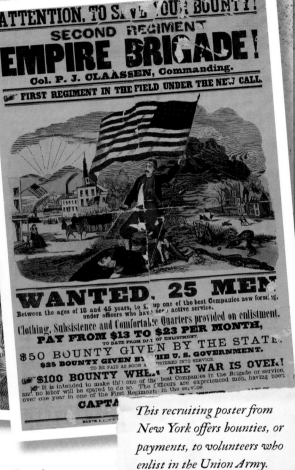

*This recruiting poster from New York offers bounties, or payments, to volunteers who enlist in the Union Army.*

The Northern plan for the war was to force the South to surrender by cutting off its supplies and taking control of the Mississippi River. The South planned to invade the North and force the U.S. government to accept its right to independence.

Northern and Southern commanders had trained together. They used the same tactics. There were few large battles during the war, but there were many minor fights, or skirmishes. Two Southern invasions of the North were defeated. Eventually, the North split the South. Union troops marched through Georgia and the Carolinas. Short of men and supplies, the South surrendered on April 9, 1865.

# Joining Up

This illustration from 1863 shows a blindfolded man choosing numbers to decide which Union men will be drafted into the army.

When the war began, the Union Army was small. The first members of the Confederate Army were Southerners who left the Union Army. Both sides relied on volunteers to swell their numbers. As fewer men joined up, both sides had to find more recruits. In the North, the length of time a soldier joined up for rose from three months to three years. In April 1862, the Confederacy began a draft system to get recruits; the Union did the same in March 1863.

> *As I lay in my bed this morning I got to thinking that I had enlisted in the Army for the period of three years. Through that time many an incident would occur and many an event take place that would be a pleasure and of much interest… I have concluded [decided] to Keep a Diary, and shall endeavor [try] to keep it as accurate as can be done…*
>
> *I have left home and a good situation… and have grasped the weapon of death for the purpose of doing my part in defending and upholding the integrity, laws and the preservation of my adopted country from a band of contemptible traitors who would if they can accomplish their hellish designs, destroy the best and noblest government on earth, merely for the purpose of benefiting themselves on the slave question.*

Prussian-born Philip Smith lived in the border state of Missouri. He volunteered for the Union Army. He wrote this diary entry on July 22, 1861.

*This recruitment poster from Delaware called for men to become skirmishers in the Union Army.*

## RECRUITMENT FACTS

- The first draft law in America was passed in the South in April 1862. All able-bodied men aged between 18 and 35 could be drafted for three years. It was later changed to men 17 to 50 years old.
- Enlistment was compulsory for Union men aged 20 to 45.
- Northerners could avoid the draft by paying a $300 fee.
- Both sides allowed men to hire a substitute to fight for them.

# Training

The 96th Pennsylvania Infantry Regiment drill at Camp Northumberland in 1861.

The recruits on both sides were mostly civilians. They had to learn to maneuver together. Their training consisted of hours of repeated drills, or military exercises, which the soldiers found boring. But drilling was meant to make the men able to move together like a machine. That would make them react automatically to commands on the battlefield, even under fire.

"The artillery, like the infantry, had its squad drill… Before field movements could be undertaken, and carried out either with much variety or success, it was indispensable for the cannoneers and [mule] drivers to be fully acquainted with their respective duties… This education included a knowledge of the ordinary routine of loading and firing, the ability to estimate distances with tolerable accuracy…

Doing this sort of business over and over again, day after day, got to be quite tedious, but it all helped to pass away the three years… One gun's crew in my company worked with such speed, strength, unanimity [togetherness], and precision that they reduced the firing to forty-nine seconds. "

John D. Billings served for three years as a private in the Union Army of the Potomac.

## TRAINING FACTS

- Drilling had been used for centuries to train groups of men to move around the battlefield.
- Soldiers practiced with their guns until they could load, fire, and reload without thinking.
- Army leaders thought that drilling helped create discipline, self-control, and a sense of teamwork.
- Both sides based their training on a manual named *Hardee's Rifle and Light Infantry Tactics* for the first two years of the war. In 1862, the manual was replaced by Silas Casey's *Infantry Tactics*.

*Union soldiers drill on a parade ground at Camp Curtin, Pennsylvania.*

# "Johnny Reb"

Although "Johnny Reb," a slang term for the average Confederate soldier, was the same nationality as his Union enemy, referred to as "Billy Yank," they were often very different. Confederate recruits were mostly farmers. They believed passionately in the South's right to make its own laws. Turning such men into soldiers was difficult. They were not used to military discipline, and found training boring.

*Private Thomas Taylor of the Confederate 8th Louisiana Regiment poses in 1861.*

**66** After a battle there was general feasting on the Confederate side. Good things, scarcely ever seen at other times, filled in the haversacks and the stomachs of the "Boys in Gray."

Imagine the feelings of men half famished when they rush into a camp… and find the coffee on the fire, sugar at hand ready to be dropped into the coffee, bread in the oven, crackers by the box, fine beef ready cooked, desiccated [dried] vegetables by the bushel, canned peaches, lobsters, tomatoes, milk, barrels of ground and roasted coffee, soda, salt, and in short everything a hungry soldier craves. **99**

Carlton McCarthy joined the Richmond Howitzers in 1864. He recalled how Confederate troops were so short of food they relied on taking it from any enemy they defeated.

## CONFEDERATE FACTS

- The Confederacy created an army a month before war began in April 1861.
- Most of the Confederate Army was made up of militiamen who volunteered to serve for 12 months.
- The main Confederate force was the Army of Northern Virginia.
- There were at least 23 separate Confederate Armies during the war.
- The Confederate Armies suffered from a lack of uniforms, weapons, and food.
- Unlike the Union Army, which had two ranks of generals, the Confederate Army had four: brigadier general, major general, lieutenant general, and (full) general.

# "Billy Yank"

**W**hen the war started, the U.S. Army had just 16,000 officers and men. By the end of the war, around 2.5 million men had served the Union. Recruitment began the day Fort Sumter surrendered to the Confederates on April 13, 1861. The Union originally relied on volunteers, but after defeats in the summer of 1862, the draft was introduced in March 1863.

*Union officers led by General George Thomas (at table) hold a council of war in Georgia in 1864.*

The 22nd New York State Militia drill at Harper's Ferry, Virginia.

66 The good steamer *Northern Bell* kept us upon the 'Father of Waters' until eleven o'clock that night. We were transferred to a train of cars immediately and started for Chicago…

All along the road through Wis., Ill., Ohio, Penn., Md, we were cheered from almost every home. The boys tired themselves more yelling than from anything they had to perform. In Pitts., we were treated to a supply of warm coffee… At every station we found old men and women ready to greet us… and in one instance an old lady, grey headed and trembling, sat in her door as we passed and blessed us so fervently that she resembled a spiritual medium passing through her gyrations [twisting movements]. 99

Jasper Newton Searles enlisted with the 1st Minnesota Infantry. He kept this account of his journey south, which began by sailing down the Mississippi, the "Father of Waters."

## U.S. ARMY FACTS

- Union soldiers first joined up for 90 days but this was raised to three years.
- Unlike Confederate soldiers, Union volunteers were paid a "bounty," or fee, for joining up.
- Each state governor was responsible for raising a certain number of men requested by the federal government.
- Union soldiers were generally better paid, fed, and clothed than their enemy.
- After the Emancipation Proclamation on January 1, 1863, recruitment of African Americans began. An estimated 186,000 African Americans served in the Union Army.

# The First Battle

*This Union newspaper illustration claims to show Confederates killing wounded Union soldiers after the battle.*

Confederate troops marched into the North. They met the Union Army at Bull Run (Manassas), just 25 miles (40 km) from the White House. Expecting an easy Union victory, many spectators rode out from Washington, D.C., to watch the battle on July 21, 1861. But the Confederates were inspired by Thomas "Stonewall" Jackson. After more soldiers arrived by railroad, the Confederates fought to victory.

"   The Federal forces were badly cut up and retreated in the most disgraceful disorder, and all on account of unskilled generalship. But, thank God, Gen. McDowell has been withdrawn and Gen. McClellan is coming to take his place… Regiment after regiment of our troops advanced up the hill in solid column towards the enemies' batteries and discharged volley after volley into the rebel ranks but every one retreated in disorder and confusion leaving many dead and dying in the field.

Every order was a blunder and every movement a failure. Had the men been left to themselves with their muskets and ammunition they could and would have done the enemy serious injury, but as it was I don't believe they killed a single rebel except what the rifles may have picked off. I am sorry, yes, I cannot but weep to tell this sickening tale of the Gallant 2nd Regiment from N.H. of which so much was expected. "

Union lieutenant Ai Thompson of the New Hampshire 2nd Regiment wrote home after the Union defeat.

## THE FIRST BATTLE FACTS

- The first major battle between the two armies was fought between July 16–22, 1861, at Manassas, Virginia.
- 35,000 Union soldiers fought under the command of General Irvin McDowell.
- Confederate General Thomas J. Jackson got his "Stonewall" nickname because he stood firm under fire.
- More than 4,500 Union and Confederate troops were killed or wounded, or were taken prisoner.
- President Lincoln asked for 100,000 new recruits after the heavy defeat.
- Lincoln fired General Irvin McDowell as commander of the Union army.

*Confederate Cavalry, led by Colonel J.E.B. Stuart, break through the Union lines on the right.*

# Battle of the Ironclads

**B**oth sides tried new technology, such as ships covered with iron armor. On March 9, 1862, the ironclads USS *Monitor* and CSS *Virginia* (formerly USS *Merrimack*) clashed at Hampton Roads. The Union built far more ships than the South. By December 1864, more than 600 Union ships blockaded Southern ports. The Confederacy used fast "blockade-runners" to outrun them.

*This print shows Union officers looking on while the* Monitor *and* Virginia *clash and a Union sailing ship sinks nearby.*

The USS Monitor (*left*) sat lower in the water than the Virginia (*right*).

> ❝ After a stormy passage, which proved us to be the finest seaboat I was ever in, we fought the *Merrimack* for more than three hours this forenoon and sent her back to Norfolk in a sinking condition. Ironclad against ironclad. We maneuvered about the bay here and went at each other with mutual fierceness. I consider that both ships were well fought. We were struck 22 times.
>
> She [CSS *Virginia*] tried to run us down and sink us, but she got the worst of it. Her bow passed over our deck and our sharp upper-edged side cut through the light iron shoe upon her stem and well into her oak. She will not try that again. She gave us a tremendous thump, but did not injure us in the least. ❞

Chief Engineer Stimers was on the USS *Monitor* when it clashed with CSS *Virginia* (*Merrimack*).

## NAVAL WAR FACTS

- Union naval strategy was based on a blockade of Southern trade.
- The Southern coastline was 3,000 miles (4,830 km) long, so it was difficult to maintain a blockade.
- The Union made the blockade more effective by capturing Southern ports.
- New technology introduced in the war included ironclad vessels and sea mines (then called torpedoes).
- Southern coastal forts had been part of U.S. coastal defenses. Their stone walls were vulnerable to shell attacks. Forts made of earth absorbed shellfire better.

# Life on Campaign

Union and Confederate soldiers all became used to living in temporary camps and marching great distances. It was common for a marching column to be over 1 mile (1.6 km) long. Soldiers carried their possessions on their backs. They built a new camp when ordered. Then they waited to fight—or to be ordered to march somewhere else.

*Union soldiers outside Petersburg, Virginia relax by playing cards and reading.*

*Soldiers in a Union camp stand in line to receive hot food. When units did not have cooks, the men took turns preparing food.*

**66** Sometimes marching orders came when least expected. I remember to have heard the long roll sounded one Saturday forenoon in the camp of the infantry that lay near us in the fall of '63. It was October 10. Our guns were [unready] for action just outside the camp where we had been lying several days utterly unsuspicious of danger.

It was quite a surprise to us; and such Lee intended it to be, he having set out to put himself between our army and Washington. We were not attacked, but started to the rear a few hours afterwards… When it was officially announced to the men on line at night that marching orders were received… those men who had not already decided the question retired to their huts in order to decide what to take and what to leave. **99**

John D. Billings was in the Union's 10th Massachusetts Volunteer Light Artillery Battery.

## CAMPAIGN FACTS

- In camp, soldiers slept in canvas A-frame or conical tents. On the road, they usually slept on the ground under a blanket and oilcloth.
- Few soldiers had comfortable shoes. Many took off their shoes on long marches and carried them slung over their shoulders.
- Soldiers often threw away blankets, overcoats, shoes, and food to avoid having to carry them on long marches.
- Sutler wagons followed Union camps selling soldiers provisions. Confederate troops were not so lucky. They were often short of food.

# Life in the Cavalry

Colonel J.E.B. Stuart leads
Confederate cavalrymen on a
famous patrol in 1862 when they
rode around a whole Union unit.

In 1860, the U.S. Army had five cavalry regiments. By the end of the war, the Union had 170 cavalry regiments. By then, the Confederates had more than 130 cavalry regiments. Union cavalry recruits were often less experienced horsemen than their enemies. They had to learn to ride after they enlisted. The more experienced Confederate horsemen specialized in large-scale mounted raids.

" I had had some experience with horses on a farm… but I had never struggled for the mastery with a fiery, untamed war-horse. Our steeds were in good condition when they arrived at the camp, and they did not get exercise enough after they came to take any of the life out of them. The first time we practiced on them with curry-comb and brush, the horses kicked us around the stables *ad libitum* [as they liked]. One recruit had all his front teeth knocked out.

But we became better acquainted with our chargers day by day, and although we started for Washington a few days after our horses had been issued, some of us attained to a confidence of our ability to manage the animals that was remarkable, considering the fact that we were thrown twice out of three times whenever we attempted to ride. "

Stanton P. Allen was 14 years old when he tried to join the Union Army. He served in the 1st Massachusetts Cavalry Regiment.

## CAVALRY FACTS

- Every cavalry regiment had its own blacksmith and farrier (person who shoed the horses).
- Confederate cavalrymen had to supply their own horses. The Union Army provided horses for their cavalry.
- As the war continued, the supply of horses in the South fell sharply.
- Cavalry raids deep into Union territory were an important tactic for raising Confederate morale.
- From 1863 the Confederate cavalry began to lose its advantage as the Union cavalry grew more experienced.

This painting shows horse-drawn artillery going into action before the Siege of Petersburg in 1865.

# In a Firefight

On April 6, 1862, 40,000 Confederate soldiers attacked unsuspecting Union soldiers near Pittsburg Landing, Shiloh, Tennessee. The Confederates caught General Ulysses S. Grant's men unawares. So many bullets buzzed through the air that one part of the battlefield became known as the Hornet's Nest. When Union reinforcements eventually arrived, the Confederates were overwhelmed.

*Union soldiers advance past their own artillery into the woods near the Hornet's Nest.*

**❝** The enemy opened on us with artillery at close range using grape, canister, and shell and all manner of deadly missiles. Above the roar of the guns could be heard the cheers of our men as they gained new ground. At last we could see the enemy and they were advancing around our left flank and the woods seemed alive with gray coats and their victorious cheer and unearthly yells and the concentrated fire which they had upon us caused somebody to give the order for retreat. The word was passed along—and we went off that bloody ground in great confusion and had to fall back over the same open ground by which we came.

As we started down the Ravine a wounded rebel caught me by the leg as I was passing and looking up at me said, 'My friend for God's sake give me a drink of water.' He had been shot about the head and was covered with blood to his feet. I at once thought of that command, 'If thine enemy thirst give him drink.' I halted and tried to get my canteen—but I could not and pulled away from him and said, 'I have not time to help you.' **❞**

Cyrus F. Boyd was in the newly formed 15th Iowa Infantry in 1861 when Union forces were surprised at Shiloh.

## SHILOH FACTS

- The battle was fought on April 6–7, 1862, at Shiloh, Tennessee, and ended in a narrow Union victory.
- Confederate General Albert Sidney Johnston was severely wounded on the first day. General Pierre G.T. Beauregard replaced him.
- The Hornet's Nest was the site of the fiercest fighting, at a sunken road near Shiloh Church.
- When Union reinforcements arrived, the 40,000 Union troops outnumbered the 30,000 Confederates.
- Total casualties numbered 23,000.

*This illustration shows Union troops (right) separated from the enemy by only a road.*

# Under Siege

*Confederates waving a white flag (top) approach Union siege lines at the end of the siege of Vicksburg.*

The war included a number of sieges in which armies surrounded enemy troops and civilians, cutting them off from supplies. This forced them to surrender through starvation or sickness. One important siege was at Vicksburg, Mississippi, in 1863. In order to gain control of the Mississippi River, Union General Ulysses S. Grant besieged Vicksburg for over 40 days.

> " I was startled by… a most fearful jar and rocking of the earth, followed by a deafening explosion, such as I had never heard before. The cave filled instantly with powder smoke and dust. I stood with a tingling, prickling sensation in my head, hands, and feet, and with a confused brain.
>
> I stepped out, to find a group of persons before my cave, looking anxiously for me; and lying all around, freshly torn, rose bushes, arbor-vitae trees, large clods of earth, splinters, pieces of plank, wood etc. A mortar shell had struck the corner of the cave, fortunately so near the brow of the hill, that it had gone obliquely into the earth, exploding as it went… sweeping all, like an avalanche, down near the entrance of my good refuge. "

Mary Loughborough was visiting her husband, a Confederate officer, when she was trapped at Vicksburg. She took shelter in a cave as Union artillery bombarded the city.

## VICKSBURG FACTS

- Grant's initial attempts to take Vicksburg in December 1862 failed.
- Grant and his Union forces laid siege to the city from May 18 until July 4, 1863.
- The Union army dug 15 miles (24 km) of trenches around Vicksburg. Using 220 heavy guns, the army bombarded the city continually.
- Many civilians hid in caves dug into the hillsides behind the city.
- By late June, there was only mule and rat meat left to eat, eventually forcing the city's surrender.

*Gunners man cannon set up in Union lines outside Petersburg during the siege of 1865.*

# The Union Home Front

*Protestors against the draft loot a store during the riots in New York City in July 1863.*

In contrast to the South, daily life in the North was not directly affected by the war. There was little fighting on Union soil, and civilians faced few shortages. Many women replaced soldiers in the workforce, however. They worked as nurses or teachers, or in government offices. Although support for the war was high, the introduction of the draft in 1863 sparked riots in New York City.

*Women fill cartridges with gunpowder and shot at a Union weapons factory.*

" July 13: Terrible Excitement throughout the City, resistance to the draft. Rows of buildings on Third Avenue burning down, also on Lexington Avenue... About 5 P.M. they appear before our factory. Charles speaks to them and with the aid of Rev. Father Mahon they draw off toward Yorkville, where late in the eve many buildings are fired. It was a terrible scene and we were of course all much exercised [anxious] at the prospect of having the factory destroyed.

July 14: Early in the morning the trouble recommences, Soldiers with Cannon marching down Third Ave… Terrible fighting between the soldiers and the mob. Col. O. Brien killed, heavy fires in the eve. Factory stopped work yesterday and today. All business in the upper part of the City suspended, Negroes [African-Americans] chased everywhere & killed when caught.

July 15: I have been unable to eat for the last 3 days except bread & drinking water for excitement. "

Piano manufacturer William Steinway kept a diary of the draft riots of July 1863. He and his employees defended the factory.

## HOME FRONT FACTS

- Before the Civil War, few women had worked. But with men away fighting, women went to work in large numbers.
- Prices increased more rapidly than wages. This caused labor strikes as workers demanded higher wages.
- The draft was introduced in March 1863.
- The biggest protest against the draft was in New York City in July 1863. Angry mobs attacked draft offices and other properties. They also murdered dozens of free African-Americans.
- The causes of the riots also included class and racial tension. Many of the rioters were Irish workers.

# Home Front in the South

When the Civil War began, Southern men and women were eager to be involved. Women planted crops, volunteered as nurses, and raised money. By 1862, however, food shortages were severe. By the time Union General William T. Sherman marched through Georgia and the Carolinas in 1865, the Confederacy was on its knees.

*Sherman's Union troops march through Georgia on his campaign against Atlanta and Savannah.*

*Southern women spin cloth to weave into uniforms for the Confederate soldiers.*

66 The pailing [fence] did not hinder them at all. They just knocked down all such like mad cattle. Right into the house, breaking open bureau drawers of all kinds faster than I could unlock. They cursed us for having hid everything and made bold threats if certain things were not brought to light, but all to no effect. They took Pa's hat and stuck him pretty badly with a bayonet to make him disclose something, but you know they were fooling with the wrong man.

Every nook and corner of the premises was searched and the things that they didn't use were burned or torn into strings. No house except the blacksmith shop was burned, but into the flames they threw every tool, plow, etc. that was on the place. The house was so crowded all day that we could scarcely move. 99

Janie Smith was the daughter of a plantation owner in North Carolina. Union troops arrived after the Battle of Averasboro in March 1865.

## HOME FRONT FACTS

- Bread riots broke out across the South in 1863 as crops ran out after a drought in summer 1862. The worst riots were in the capital, Richmond, Virginia.
- Union commanders wanted Sherman to "squeeze the South."
- Sherman invaded Georgia in May 1864 and captured the capital, Atlanta, in September. He captured Savannah, on the coast, in December. He then headed into South and North Carolina.
- Sherman's march left 250,000 Southern families as refugees.
- Sherman treated South Carolina particularly harshly, because it was the first state to leave the Union.

# The African-American Experience

I n July 1862, Congress passed two new laws to allow African-Americans to enlist in the Union armies. Within weeks, black soldiers were joining throughout the Union and in captured Confederate territory. They served in all-black regiments commanded by white officers.

*The 4th Colored Infantry were formed in Maryland at the start of 1863. They served in Virginia and North Carolina.*

**❝** All over the camp the lights glimmer in the tents, and as I sit at my desk in the open doorway, there come mingled sounds of stir and glee. Boys laugh and shout. A feeble flute stirs somewhere in some tent, not an officer's. A drum throbs far away in another. Wild kildeer-plover [birds] flit and wail above us, like the haunting souls of dead slave-masters. And from a neighboring cook-fire comes the monotonous sound of that strange festival, half pow-wow, half prayer-meeting, which they know only as a 'shout.' These fires are usually enclosed in a little booth, made neatly of palm-leaves and covered in at top, a regular native African hut…

This hut is now crammed with men, singing at the top of their voices… all accompanied with a regular drumming of the feet and clapping of the hands, like castanets. **❞**

The white abolitionist Thomas W. Higginson commanded the 1st South Carolina Volunteers from September 1862.

## AFRICAN-AMERICAN FACTS

- White Union soldiers were paid an average of $13 a month, but black soldiers got only $10 a month.
- White soldiers received a bonus upon enlisting; black soldiers did not.
- Many white soldiers were prejudiced against serving with black soldiers.
- The Confederates treated all captured black soldiers as runaway slaves.
- The Union Navy admitted African-Americans from the start of the war.
- On March 13, 1865, the Confederate Congress passed a law allowing the use of black troops.

*Nimrod Burke was a scout for the U.S. Army until he joined the 23rd Regiment of Colored Infantry in 1864.*

# The Bloodiest Day

Union troops (left) attack Confederate lines near Burnside's Bridge at Antietam.

The Battle of Antietam (Sharpsburg) was the bloodiest single day of the war. It was the end of Confederate General Robert E. Lee's first invasion of the North. Union General George B. McClellan learned of Lee's plan to invade Maryland. He also knew the Confederate forces were divided. McClellan used this knowledge to stop Lee's advance.

**❝** On the right and the left my men were falling under the death-dealing crossfire like trees in a hurricane… Both sides stood in the open at short range and without the semblance of breastworks, and the firing was doing a deadly work.

Higher up in the same leg I was again shot; but still no bone was broken. I was able to walk along the line and give encouragement to my resolute riflemen, who were firing with the coolness and steadiness of peace soldiers in target practice… A fourth ball ripped through my shoulder, leaving its base and wad of clothing in its track. I could still stand and walk, although the shocks and loss of blood had left but little of my normal strength. **❞**

Colonel John B. Gordon of the Confederate 6th Alabama Infantry, Rhodes's Brigade, was seriously injured at Bloody Lane, Antietam.

## ANTIETAM FACTS

- The battle was fought on September 16–18, 1862 at Antietam, Maryland.
- The battle was a strategic victory for the Union, as the Confederate invasion of the North was halted.
- There were a total of 22,400 casualties.
- Fighting continued for four hours at a sunken road known as "Bloody Lane."
- After the battle, President Lincoln issued his preliminary Emancipation Proclamation. It promised to free slaves in the South.

*After the North's tactical victory, President Lincoln (in tall hat, center) visits his generals at Antietam.*

# The Battle of Gettysburg

The battle of Gettysburg, fought from July 1-3, 1863, was the largest battle of the war. It occurred during General Robert E. Lee's second invasion of the North. At the battle's height, Lee sent General George C. Pickett to lead some 12,500 troops against Union positions. Pickett's Charge ended in disaster, and Lee retreated.

*Union troops commanded by General Winfield Scott Hancock rally to fight off Pickett's Charge.*

*Confederates (left) face Union cannon in a doomed attempt to capture the key position of Little Round Top.*

66 You will want me to tell you of the battle. It was awful. Language will not convey an idea. We were not under fire until 2 or 3 o'clock in the afternoon. We then got under a fierce artillery fire, but with no damage.

We then moved to another position near a peach orchard. Then under another heavy fire that made the earth tremble and the air shook and was so full of smoke you could not see. A good many of our Regt. were shot here…

The loss of our Corps is 4,600, or about one-half. I went over the battlefield before the men were buried and they lay awful thick, I can assure you… In one place I counted 16 in a spot no larger than your kitchen. It was a hard sight. 99

Private John Burrill fought at Gettysburg with the Union Second New Hampshire Volunteers.

## GETTYSBURG FACTS

- The battle was fought between July 1–3, 1863, after 75,000 Confederate and 90,000 Union troops met by chance at Gettysburg, Pennsylvania.
- Lee's initial attack was driven back. He later suffered heavy losses during Pickett's Charge.
- Total casualties were 28,000 Confederates and 23,000 Union troops.
- Lee blamed himself for the defeat and tried unsuccessfully to resign.
- Four months later, President Lincoln visited the battlefield and made his Gettysburg Address. It is one of the most famous speeches ever made.

# Medicine and Nursing

*Volunteer nurse Anne Bell looks after wounded soldiers in a Union hospital.*

**M**edicine during the Civil War was not very advanced. Hospitals were unhygienic. There were no antibiotics, so soldiers often died from infection as well as during surgery. More men died from disease than from combat wounds. Many women volunteered to serve as nurses. In many ways, the conflict marked the start of modern nursing.

*A surgeon performs an operation in the open air. Many patients died from either shock or infection.*

66 In they came, some on stretchers, some in men's arms, some feebly staggering along propped up on rude [basic] crutches, and one lay stark and still with covered face, as a comrade gave his name to be recorded before they carried him away to the dead house.

All was hurry and confusion; the hall was full of these wrecks of humanity, for the most exhausted could not reach a bed till duly ticketed and registered; the walls were lined with rows of such as could not sit, the floor covered with the more disabled…

The sight of several stretchers, each with its legless, armless, and desperately wounded occupant, entering my ward, admonished [reminded] me that I was there to work, so I corked up my feelings. 99

Louisa May Alcott, the author of *Little Women*, worked as a Union nurse.

## MEDICINE FACTS

- At the start of war, the U.S. Army had just 113 surgeons. Of them, 24 resigned to support the Confederacy.
- The wounded were treated in field hospitals or taken to city hospitals.
- Cramped, dirty conditions made it easier for diseases to spread.
- Chloroform was used as an anesthetic to make operations less painful.
- The South lacked medicines. During surgery, soldiers drank whiskey to kill the pain, and bit on a bullet.
- Dorothea Dix organized a Union nursing service. Clara Barton and Louisa May Alcott both volunteered to join it.

# Recreation and Entertainment

To avoid homesickness and boredom when they were not in battle, soldiers read and wrote letters. The Bible was the most popular book, but 25-cent thrillers and picture books were also popular. Soldiers also played cards, checkers, and chess, or made music. Popular sports included baseball, wrestling, and wheelbarrow racing.

*Union prisoners of war play baseball in Salisbury, North Carolina, in 1863.*

Men of the 114th Pennsylvania Infantry play cards near their tents at Petersburg in August 1864.

## RECREATION FACTS

- Letter writing was a lifeline, and more Americans than ever could read and write.
- Music-making was also popular. Many units had brass or fife and drum bands.
- Baseball, which was still a new sport, was widely played.
- During the winter, snowball fights were often held. They could include whole regiments or brigades.
- Soldiers carved pipes from briarroot and turned sea shells and bones into rings and ornaments.
- Gambling was common among soldiers on both sides.

" Two lines of battle were formed by the 10 & 44 Regts. which charged the camp of the 41st Miss. The result of the battle was the dispersion of the 41st, who for a short time fought stubbornly [against] the capture of their Colonel and several other officers and the occupation of their Regimental Parade [ground]…

Many unsuccessful attempts were made by the foe to pass the bridge [to the camp] and cross the stream lower down. Discouraged by their repeated failures they finally withdrew altogether. In the afternoon they again advanced upon our camp, having previously made an insolent demand for the unconditional surrender of the army of the East, as we were called, allowing us but ten minutes to decide. The demand being refused, a hot attack was made and after the engagement of a half or three quarters of an hour terminated in their repulse. "

Captain T. Otis Baker of the 10th Mississippi Infantry describes a snowball fight in his Confederate camp on March 22, 1864.

# Discipline and Punishment

**M**aintaining discipline was a problem for both sides during the Civil War. Many civilian volunteers found it hard to obey strict military rules. Common breaches of army rules included getting drunk, falling asleep on duty, fighting, and stealing from other soldiers. Desertion and cowardice were much more serious offenses. They were often punishable by death.

*Private William Johnson is executed by firing squad for deserting the Union Army in December 1861.*

*A soldier is punished by "riding the rail," or sitting for a long period on a thin or ridged pole.*

" One morning, about daybreak, the new guard was relieving the old guard. It was a bitter cold morning, and on coming to our extreme outpost, I saw a soldier—he was but a mere boy—either dead or asleep at his post. The sergeant commanding the relief [new guard] went up to him and shook him. He immediately woke up and seemed very much frightened. He was fast asleep at his post. The sergeant had him arrested.

I was summoned to appear as a witness against him for being asleep at his post in the enemy's country. An example had to be made of someone. He had to be tried for his life. The court-martial was made up of seven or eight officers [from] a different regiment. The witnesses all testified against him, charges and specifications were read, and by the rules of war he had to be shot to death by musketry [firing squad]… [But] he was acquitted [released], and I was glad of it. "

Confederate soldier Sam Rush Watkins served in the First Tennessee Infantry. He recalls a court martial.

## DISCIPLINE FACTS

- Union commanders blamed the defeat at Bull Run (Manassas) on July 21, 1861 on a lack of discipline among Union troops.
- Fighting or drunkenness was punished by imprisonment in a guardhouse on a ration of bread and water.
- Drunkenness could also be punished by making a soldier stand on a barrel with a bottle of whiskey around his neck.
- Thieves were marched around camp wearing a sign that read, "Thief."
- The Confederate Army of Northern Virginia executed 31 men for desertion during the last six months of the war.

# Lee's Surrender

Even after the fall of the Confederate capital, Richmond, on April 2, 1865, the Confederates were reluctant to surrender. But after heavy losses at the Battle of Sayler's Creek on April 7, General Robert E. Lee asked Union General Grant to accept his surrender. This took place at Appomattox Court House on April 9, 1865.

General Lee (left) signs the Confederate surrender, watched by General Grant (sitting, right) and his generals.

*Confederate soldiers roll up their flag for the last time after Lee's surrender at Appomattox.*

" I felt like anything rather than rejoicing at the downfall of a foe who had fought so long and valiantly, and had suffered so much for a cause, though that cause was, I believe, one of the worst for which a people ever fought, and one for which there was the least excuse …

General Lee was dressed in a full uniform which was entirely new, and was wearing a sword of considerable value, very likely the sword which had been presented by the State of Virginia; at all events, it was a different sword from the one that would be worn in the field. In my rough traveling suit, the uniform of a private with the straps of a lieutenant-general, I must have contrasted very strangely with a man so handsomely dressed, six feet high and of faultless form. "

In his memoirs, General Ulysses S. Grant recalls meeting with General Robert E. Lee at the Appomattox Court House.

## SURRENDER FACTS

- Lee lost 8,000 men—a quarter of his men—at the Battle of Sayler's Creek, and realized that he had to surrender.
- Grant did not impose harsh surrender terms. He allowed Lee's men to go home, and let the soldiers keep their horses.
- When the Confederate troops laid down their arms, their Union opponents gave them a guard of honor.
- Confederate president Jefferson Davis was arrested on May 10 while trying to escape capture.
- The last Confederate Army did not surrender until June 23, 1865.

# The Death of Lincoln

*This illustration shows John Wilkes Booth shooting Lincoln in the theater.*

The happiness felt in the North after Lee's surrender was brief. On the night of April 14, 1865, a Southern supporter named John Wilkes Booth shot President Lincoln at a theater in Washington, D.C. Lincoln died of his injuries the next day. The task of reconstructing (or rebuilding) the country was left to the vice-president, Andrew Johnson, who wanted to admit the Southern states back into the Union.

*Union troops march down Pennsylvania Avenue in Washington, D.C., in a grand review in May 1865.*

66 Large groups of people were gathered, all anxious and solicitous. Some one or more from each group stepped forward as I passed, to inquire into the condition of the President, and to ask if there was no hope. Intense grief was on every countenance when I replied that the President could survive but a short time. The colored people especially—and there were at this time more of them, perhaps, than the whites—were overwhelmed with grief.

A little before seven, I went into the room where the dying President was rapidly drawing near the closing moments. His wife soon after made her last visit to him. The death struggle had begun.

The respiration of the President became suspended at intervals, and at last entirely ceased at twenty-two minutes past seven. 99

Gideon Welles, Secretary of the Navy, witnessed Abraham Lincoln's final moments.

## RECONSTRUCTION FACTS

- Reconstruction is the name given to the period from 1865 to 1877.
- In January 1865, the Thirteenth Amendment abolished slavery.
- Congress passed the Civil Rights Act in April 1866. It said that all persons born in the United States were citizens, regardless of their race.
- Tennessee was readmitted to the Union in 1866.
- The states of Arkansas, North Carolina, South Carolina, Louisiana, Alabama, and Florida were readmitted in 1868.
- Virginia, Mississippi, Texas, and Georgia were readmitted in 1870.

# GLOSSARY

**abolitionist** A person who campaigned against slavery.

**antibiotic** A medicine that prevents or clears up infection.

**blockade** Sealing off an area to prevent goods or people from leaving or entering.

**bounty** A payment received for volunteering for military service.

**court-martial** A legal court that judges soldiers accused of breaking military law.

**desertion** Leaving one's post without permission.

**draft** The process of selecting individuals for military service.

**drill** Training in military maneuvers through repeated exercises.

**enlistment** Joining up for military service.

**guard of honor** A group of soldiers who perform a ceremony.

**ironclad** A warship whose surfaces are coated in armor plates.

**morale** The belief of a fighting force that it will eventually be victorious.

**Reconstruction** The name given to the period after the Civil War, when the Union was reunited.

**siege** A military operation in which an area is cut off from supplies and forced to surrender.

**skirmish** A small-scale fight between small groups of soldiers.

**strategic** Connected with the long-term outcome of a war rather than the immediate fighting.

**substitute** A man paid to perform military service in place of the man who was drafted to do it.

**sutler** A trader who followed an army to sell food and drink to the soldiers.

# FURTHER INFORMATION

## Books

Anderson, Tanya. *Tillie Pierce: Teen Eyewitness to the Battle of Gettysburg.* Twenty-First Century, 2013.

Ford, Carin T. *An Overview of the American Civil War Through Primary Sources* (Civil War Through Primary Sources). Enslow Publishers, 2013.

Hyslop, Steve. *Eyewitness to the Civil War.* National Geographic Society, 2006.

McDonald, Archie P. *Primary Source Accounts of the Civil War* (America's Wars Through Primary Sources). Myreportlinks.com, 2006.

Samuels, Charlie. *Timeline of the Civil War* (Americans at War). Gareth Stevens Publishing, 2011.

Stanchak, John. *Eyewitness Civil War* (DK Eyewitness Books). DK Publishing, 2011.

## Websites

**www.eyewitnesstohistory.com/ cwfrm.htm**
Links to numerous first-hand accounts from the Eyewitness to History website.

**www.historyplace.com/civilwar/**
An interactive timeline of the Civil War from The History Place™.

**www.civilwar.si.edu/**
An exploration of the Civil War through the collections of the Smithsonian Institution.

**www.history.com/topics/american-civil-war**
History.com index for its many Civil War pages.

**Publisher's note to educators and parents:** Our editors have carefully reviewed these websites to ensure that they are suitable for students. Many websites change frequently, however, and we cannot guarantee that a site's future contents will continue to meet our high standards of quality and educational value. Be advised that students should be closely supervised whenever they access the Internet.

# INDEX

abolitionists 31
African Americans 13, 30–31
Alcott, Louisa May 37
Antietam, Battle of 32–33
Appomattox Courthouse 42–43
Army of Northern Virginia 11

baseball 38, 39
battles
    Antietam 32–33
    First Bull Run 4, 14–15
    Gettysburg 34–35
    Hampton Roads 16–17
    Shiloh 22–23
"Billy Yank" 12–13
blockade 16, 17
Booth, John Wilkes 44
boredom 38
bread riots 29
Bull Run, First Battle of 4, 14–15, 41

campaigning 18–19
cavalry 20–21
civilians 25, 26–27, 28–29
Civil Rights Act 45
clothes 19
Confederate Army 6, 7, 10–11
Confederate States of America 4
cowardice 40

Davis, Jefferson 43
desertion 40
discipline 40–41
Dix, Dorothea 37
draft 6, 7, 12, 26
draft riots 26–27
drills 8, 9

Emancipation Proclamation 13, 33
enlistment 7
execution 40, 41

food 11, 19, 28
Fort Sumter 12

gambling 39
Georgia 28, 29
Gettysburg, Battle of 34–35
Gettysburg Address 35
Grant, Ulysses S. 22, 24, 25, 42, 43

Hampton Roads, battle of 16–17
*Hardee's Rifle and Light Infantry Tactics* 9
home front, Southern 28–29
home front, Union 26–27

ironclads 16–17

Jackson, Thomas Stonewall 14, 15
"Johnny Reb" 10–11
Johnson, Andrew 44
Johnston, Albert Sidney 23

Lee, Robert E. 32, 34, 35, 42, 43
letters 38, 39
Lincoln, Abraham 4, 33, 44–45
living conditions 18–19

McClellan, George B. 32
McDowell, Irvin 15
medical care 36–37
*Merrimack*, 16–17
Mississippi River 5, 13, 24
*Monitor*, USS 16–17
morale 21

naval war 16–17
New York City 26–27
North Carolina 29
nursing 36–37

Pickett's Charge 34, 35
Pittsburg Landing 22

reading 38
Reconstruction 44–45
recreation 38–39
recruitment 12, 13
Richmond 42

Sherman, General William T. 28
Shiloh, Battle of 22–23
sieges 24–25
slavery 4
slaves 31
South Carolina 4, 28, 29
sports 38
strategy, Union 5
surgery 36, 37
surrender, South 5, 42–43

technology 16
tents 19
thieves 41
Thirteenth Amendment 45
training 8–9, 10

Union Army 6–7, 9, 12–13

Vicksburg 24–25

women 26, 27, 36